Blockchain Technology
I told you so!

What Bitcoins, Ethereum and other
blockchain technologies are and how
you can use them for fun and profit

(Tom J. Bernstein)

Blockchain Technology - I told you so!
What Bitcoins, Ethereum and other blockchain technologies
are and how you can use them for fun and profit

ISBN-13: 978-1981819928
ISBN-10: 1981819924

Contents

Introduction

The blockchain technology has become very popular. It was initially designed and developed to be used for Bitcoin cryptocurrency. However, it has been discovered that this technology can be applied to several other areas, leading to its rising popularity. The fact that blockchain technology provides its users with a distributed ledger, which does not need a centralized authority to maintain, has made it a technology of interest for most industries in various sectors of the economy.

With blockchain technology, some level of anonymity is provided to users. This is because it doesn't require their personal data to transact using some of the technologies such as Bitcoin. Most people want to stay anonymous when browsing the Internet. Bitcoin helps make this a reality.

Most people have heard about blockchain technology. However, they do not know what exactly it is, or how and where it can be used. This book discusses everything to do with blockchain technology. Enjoy reading!

Chapter 1- What is Blockchain?

The blockchain technology is the brainchild of a person or a group of people known as Satoshi Nakamoto. Since its discovery, blockchain has greatly evolved to become something else. It allows for the distribution of digital information but this information cannot be copied. It has created the backbone for a new type of Internet. Blockchain technology was initially devised for Bitcoin, a digital currency, but this technology is now being uses in various areas.

Bitcoin has been referred to as "digital gold". To date, the currency has a total value of up to $9 billion. US. blockchains are capable of making other types of digital currency. Similar to the Internet, you don't to know how the blockchain operates to use it. However, it is good for you to have sufficient knowledge about this technology to know why the technology is called revolutionary.

The blockchain is simply a decentralized, digitized, public ledger recording of all cryptocurrency transactions. It grows constantly as new and completed blocks are added to it chronologically. With blockchain technology, market participants are able to keep track of digital currency transactions without the need for central recordkeeping. Currently, it is used for the verification of transactions, but it is possible to code, digitize then insert any document into the blockchain. When this is done, an incredible unchangeable record will be created. The authenticity of records in a blockchain can be verified by the entire community instead of using a centralized authority.

The "block" is the current part of the blockchain responsible for recording some or all recent transactions. Once the block is completed, it will be added to the blockchain in the form of a permanent database. After a block is completed, a new one must be generated where writing of current transactions will take place. The blockchain has countless number of blocks connected to each other in a linear and chronological order. Each block has a hash of the previous block. The blockchain is aware of each user address from the first block to the most recent one. The transactions are immutable, meaning they can't be deleted. The addition of blocks is done using cryptography to ensure they are meddle-proof--that the data can only be distributed and not copied.

The blockchain is not much different from the things you are used to such as Wikipedia. In the blockchain, many users are allowed to write information into a record, and the changes and updates done to that record are controlled by a community of users. The entries in a Wikipedia are not the product of a single publisher. No single individual is responsible for controlling entries. The two, Wikipedia and blockchain, run on a distributed network, which is the Internet.

However, the Wikipedia is built on the World Wide Web (WWW) by use of the client-server network model. A user whose account has permission is allowed to change the entries, which are normally kept in a centralized server. The user is always provided with the updated page, or the Master copy. There are Wikipedia administrators tasked with the responsibility of controlling access and permission to the entries.

Blockchain creates a different digital backbone due to the use of a distributed database. This forms its most unique and important feature: each network node updates the record independently, and the most popular record becomes the de facto official record; and all nodes end up with the same conclusion.

In the blockchain, transactions are normally broadcast, with each node creating its own version of updated events. Thus, there is no need for a trusted party in the blockchain who can be tasked with the responsibility of facilitating the digital relationships.

Digital Trust in Blockchain

In digital operations, trust involves proving identity (authenticity) and proving permission (authorization). The goal is to determine whether a user is who they claim to be and whether they are allowed to do what they need to do. In blockchain technology, private key cryptography is employed to implement the authentication mechanism. With a private key, one doesn't need to share more information about themselves for an exchange. The blockchain relies on a peer-to-peer, distributed network as a way of avoiding the problems associated with a centralized failure.

The distributed network should be committed to the security and recordkeeping of the transaction network. Authorization of transaction on the whole network results from the application of rules according to which it was designed. When authorization and authentication are used in this way in the digital world, there is no need for the reliance on trust. Companies and organizations from all over the world are aware of the technology, and they are turning to it because it is cheap.

The concept of shared ledgers and cryptographic keys can incentivize users to formalize and secure digital relationships. Banks, governments and IT firms are looking for ways to build this transaction layer. Authorization and authentication, which are very vital in digital transactions, are established after the configuration of the blockchain technology. It is an idea applicable to any need for a trustworthy system of records.

Chapter 2- How does Blockchain work?

Blockchain technology may be termed the best technology since the invention of the Internet. It facilitates value exchange without the need for a central authority or trust. Suppose you and I bet $100 on tomorrow's weather in New York City. I bet it will be rainy and you bet it will be sunny. There are three options how this transaction can be managed:

1. We can choose to *trust* each other. The one who loses will give $100 to the winner. This is a good way of managing the transaction if we are friends. However, it is easy for one to fail to pay the other.
2. We can choose to turn the bet into a *contract*. When the contract is put into place, it will be easy for both parties to pay. However, if any of the parties fails to pay, the winner will incur extra charges to cover legal expenses and the verdict may take a long time. This is not an optimal way of managing the transaction, especially if the amount involved is small.
3. We can choose to involve a neutral third party. Each gives $100 to the third party, and the whole amount ($200) will be given to the winner. However, the

third party can run away with the money, and we remain with our first two options.

The trust and contract options are not optimal solutions. It is impossible for us to trust strangers, and creating a contract requires the expenditure of both time and money. The blockchain is the best alternative since it provides us with a quick, secure and cheap way of managing.

The blockchain allows us to write a small piece of code, a programming running on the blockchain to which we will each send $100. The program will keep the $200 very securely and use automatic means to check tomorrow's weather from various sources. The whole amount ($200) will be sent to the winner. Each party is in a position to check the logic of the contract, and when it is running on the blockchain, no one is allowed to stop or even change it. For $100, this logic can be expensive or even tiresome to implement, but it will be good for costly transactions like selling a house.

The most common and popular application of the Blockchain technology is the Bitcoin, simply a digital currency one can use for the exchange of products and services, just like the Euro, USD and others. This application of the blockchain can help us understand better how it works.

With Bitcoin, an Internet user can transfer a unique piece of digital information to another user in such a way as to guarantee that the transfer is safe and secure. Everybody is aware that the transfer has taken place, and no one can question its legitimacy.

One Bitcoin is simply a single unit of Bitcoin (BTC) digital currency, and it has no value by itself just like the dollar. It only acquires value because we have agreed to trade both goods and services for some higher amount of currency that is under our control, and our belief is that others will do the same.

The blockchain uses a ledger to help us know the amount of Bitcoin each of us owns. A ledger is simply a digital file which keeps track of all Bitcoin transactions. The ledger in this case is not stored in a central entity server like in a bank, but is distributed across the world via a network of private computers which store data and at the same time execute computations. Each of thes computers is referred to as a *node* in the network and has a copy of the ledger file.

If Bob needs to send Bitcoins to Alice, he must distribute a message across the network stating the amount of Bitcoins by which his account must be reduced, say 10, and the amount of Bitcoins in Alice's account should rise by the same amount, that is, 10. Each node in the network will receive this message, and they will apply the changes to their copy of the ledger file and the account balances will be updated. Each node will pass the message to nearby nodes.

The ledger in this case is maintained by a group of computers rather than by a centralized entity. This has a number of implications:

1. In the banking system, we are only able to know our transactions and account balances. In the blockchain, everyone can see the transactions of others.
2. While you are able to trust a bank, Bitcoin is naturally distributed; and in case something goes wrong, there will be no anyone to sue or any help desk to call.
3. The blockchain network has been designed in such a way that there is no need for trust, reliability and security as they are achieved through code and special mathematical functions.

The blockchain can be defined as a system that allows for a group of connected computers, some single to secure and update ledgers. For one to be in a position to perform any transactions on the blockchain, they must have a *wallet*. This is simply program that allows one to store and exchange their Bitcoins. Since one is allowed to spend only their own coins, each wallet must be protected by a special cryptographic method that uses a pair of different connected keys: a private and a public key.

If a public key is used for encryption of a particular message, the message can only be decrypted and read by the owner of the paired private key. When Bob needs to send a message, he must encrypt it using the private key of his wallet before broadcasting it. This means that he will be the only one capable of spending the Bitcoins he owns. This is because he (Bob) is the one who knows his private key, which is necessary for his wallet to be unlocked. For the nodes in the network to verify if a particular transaction comes from him, they must decrypt it using the public key of Bob's wallet.

When one is using the private key of their wallet to encrypt a transaction, a digital signature will be generated and used for the purpose of checking or verifying transactions on the blockchain. A digital signature is simply a string of text which results after combing your transaction request and private key, meaning that it cannot be used for any other transactions. If a single character in the transaction request is changed, the digital signature will also change, making it hard for any attacker to alter your transaction request or the amount of Bitcoins you need to send.

For you to be able to send Bitcoins, you must prove that you own the private key of the wallet since you will have to use it to encrypt the transaction request message. The message can only broadcast after it has been encrypted, and you don't have to reveal your private key.

The question is, how can you know your account balance? The blockchain system does not track the balances for the accounts, but only records the transactions requested. Instead of keeping the balances, it only keeps the transactions broadcast over the Bitcoin network. For you to know the balance on your account, you must analyze all the transactions that have happened on the network that are connected directly to your wallet. This is facilitated by the fact that there are links to previous transactions. For Alice to send 10 Bitcoins to Bob, she must generate a transaction request which includes the links to previous incoming transactions whose total balance is either equal to or more than 10 Bitcoins.

The links are referred to as inputs, and the network nodes will verify whether the total amount of Bitcoins equals or exceeds 10 Bitcoins and that the inputs are yet to be spent. Note that once inputs are referenced in a particular transaction, these will not be considered as valid in any future transactions.

Chapter 3- What Problems does Blockchain Technology Solve?

A lot is being said about the blockchain technology, but the question is, what problems does the blockchain really solve?

Computer databases are unable to talk to each other without a layer of expensive fault-prone human administration or a bureaucratic central authority that controls every node. The blockchain solves this problem. The blockchain is a single decentralized database managed by software and at the same time shared by many users without a third party authority. With this, the processing of transactions is less error-prone and costly. The software increases processing efficiency since new links can be created as needed, and the efficiency of management will be improved since no gatekeepers will be needed. The blockchain can be applied anywhere many people need to interact with a computer database.

Centralization

Traditionally, for databases to communicate with each other, one has to consolidate and combine them into a single database, assuming that there will enough commonality between the databases to make it possible to patch them together. This is a typical approach for acquisitions and mergers of corporations in which two almost similar entities combine their data under a central authority. This leads to increased efficiency and elimination of redundancy. However, centralization can lead to a monopoly, top-heavy hierarchy, stagnation, obfuscation and vulnerability to external shocks. In case failures occur, blanket legislation and government regulations will be triggered. Despite all this, the problem will remain, that is, how can the mega-databases communicate with other mega-databases?

Decentralization

Sharing of one database can help eliminate intermediaries and share data between organizations. Multiple users can access and populate the database simultaneously without controls, centralized authority or a consensus. Natural organic links will form, and operations will become faster, easy and cheaper to perform and maintain. The network effect can apply such that the network value will grow exponentially. However, one will not have a way of stopping a person from cheating another, altering the conditions of the contract, or double spending on some unit account. Blockchain technology helps solve the problems associated with decentralized databases.

Before Bitcoin, after sending a contract by email, each party involved would have to hold an identical copy that can be manipulated easily. After the invention of Bitcoin, individuals are able to send contracts electronically, and the recipient will only have to hold the valid copy. This can be a difficult task for a computer. However, it can help the computers perform all the functions of the administrators in nearly each of their interactions.

Centralized databases are known for their low scalability. Blockchain is capable of scaling in a bid to handle large and complex transactions. It is also good in scaling down to handle billions of micro-transactions with only a little difference in operating costs.

Blockchain technology has enabled business deals that might otherwise have never become viable. The technology has the potential to eliminate a tremendous amount of friction from everyday agreements and transactions.

Chapter 4- History of Blockchain Technology

The origin of the Blockchain is the 9-page whitepaper published by an anonymous scientist named Satoshi Nakamoto in the year 2008. The paper shows how to make a completely novel cryptocurrency based on some sophisticated mathematical formula together with a resilient distributed architecture.

The publication described in detail how one can use Bitcoin to send payments between willing entities with no need for a third-party financial body. The storage of the transactions is done in a blockchain ledger, and a digital signature iss used to link the network block to preceding ones. To ensure that trust is achieved in the ledger, the network participants can run complex algorithms to authenticate the signatures and add transactions to blockchain.

Blockchain technology allows individuals who don't trust each other or who are strangers to each other to exchange value over cyberspace. By the year 2014, there were over 80 uses of such crypto-ledgers. This is what has happened in the past 10 years:

- The first innovation of the blockchain was Bitcoin, a digital currency experiment. Bitcoin has a market cap ranging between $10-$20 billion dollars, and millions of people use it for payments, including the large and growing remittance business.
- The second innovation was the blockchain, operating on the knowledge that the underlying technology used by Bitcoin could be separated from currency and used for all types of other inter-organizational cooperation. Nearly all financial organizations in the world are doing research on blockchain technology. 17% of banks are expected to implement the technology in their operations by 2017.
- The third innovation was the "smart contract", built into a second generation blockchain system named Ethereum. It built small computer programs into the blockchain to allow financial instruments like loans and bonds to be represented rather than using cash-like tokens only such as Bitcoin. Currently, the Ethereum smart contract platform has a market cap of about a billion dollars, and hundreds of projects are headed towards the market.
- The fourth innovation was the "proof of stake", the current cutting edge of blockchain thinking. The "proof of work" system is responsible for securing the current generation blockchains, whereby the group

with the largest total computing power will be responsible for making decisions. The groups are known as "miners" and they operate huge data centers to provide security in exchange for cryptocurrency payments. In new systems, the data centers have been removed and replaced with complex financial instruments for the same or even a higher degree of security.

- The fifth innovation is blockchain scaling. Currently in the blockchain, each computer located in the network has to process each transaction. This process is slow. With a scaled blockchain, the process can be accelerated, without sacrificing security, by determining the number of computers necessary for a transaction to be validated and dividing the work in an efficient manner. It becomes difficult for one to manage this without negatively affecting the legendary and robustness of the blockchain. However, the problem is not intractable. A scaled blockchain should be fast to power the Internet of Things (IoT), then go head-to-head with most payment middlemen (SWIFT and VISA) of the world.

The above innovative steps for the last 10 years represent the work of an elite group of cryptographers, computer scientists and mathematicians. The blockchain is full of potential, and a lot is expected to happen in the future. Drones and self-driving cars will use the blockchain to pay for some services such as landing pads and charging stations. International currency transfers are expected to take hours from days, then minutes, and this will provide a higher degree of reliability compared to the current system. These changes and many others are expected to lower transaction costs.

Chapter 5- How is Blockchain Related to Bitcoin?

Bitcoin and Blockchain are not the same. However, the two closely related. When the open source code for Bitcoin was released, the blockchain was wrapped in it. Bitcoin forms the first Blockchain application, and due to this, people have used "Bitcoin" to refer to "blockchain".

Bitcoin is an unregulated digital currency developed in 2008 by Satoshi Nakamoto. It was developed for the purpose of making online transactions simple avoiding government regulations on currencies. The cryptocurrency helped to do away with intermediaries during online transactions. Accomplishing this required more than just money. A secure way of doing transactions with the cryptocurrency was needed.

Bitcoin transactions are normally transferred and stored in distributed ledgers on a peer-to-peer network that is public, open and anonymous. The Blockchain is the underlying technology on which the ledger runs.

How the Bitcoin Blockchain Works

The Bitcoin blockchain is simply a database or ledger made up of Bitcoin transaction records. However, since there is no central authority and the database is distributed across a peer-to-peer network, the participating nodes must have a way of agreeing on the validity of transactions before they can be recorded. This agreement is known as a "consensus" and it is achieved through a process known as "mining".

Once someone has used Bitcoins, miners are engaged in complex, resource-intensive computational equations in a bid to verify legitimacy of the transactions. Through the mining process, a "proof of work" that meets some specific requirements is created. It is simply a piece of code that is time-consuming and costly to produce but that others can easily verify.

For a transaction to be considered as valid on the blockchain, the individual record should have a proof of work so as to prove that a consensus had been reached. This way, it is hard to tamper with transaction records or change them after they have been added to the blockchain.

How is it Different from Blockchain for Business?

The Bitcoin blockchain was specifically designed and developed for use with cryptocurrency. This explains the reason it took some time for people to realize that this technology can be applied to other areas. Also, one has to modify the technology so that it can meet the needs of business. There are three main characteristics that differentiate the Bitcoin blockchain from the blockchain for business. Let's explore them:

1. Assets over cryptocurrency

   Blockchain can be used for a wide range of assets other than cryptocurrency alone. Tangible assets like real estate, cars and food items, and intangible assets such securities, private equities and bonds, are a fair game.

2. Identity over Anonymity

   Bitcoin only thrives because of anonymity. Everyone is allowed to look at the ledger to know if any transaction has happened, but the account information is simply a sequence of meaningless numbers. Businesses have AML (anti-money laundering) and KYC (know your customer) requirements that help them to know exactly with whom they are transacting. Business network participants require the polar opposite of anonymity, that is, privacy.

3. Selective endorsement over proof of work
   In blockchain for business, consensus is not achieved through mining but through a process known as "selective endorsement". They need to be in a position to determine who verifies transactions in the same way as it is done today in business. In Bitcoin, this is done differently since the entire network must work in a bid to verify transactions.

Chapter 6- Managing Digital Transactions

Blockchain technology is capable of disrupting multiple technologies including supply chain management, digital rights management, cybersecurity and others. The technology is capable of tracing transactions and maintaining an immutable record, and this can greatly change how transactions are done today. The blockchain removes the need for a mediator when carrying out transactions and it brings the two transacting parties together without the issue of mistrust. Validation of transactions normally happens once the two ends have completed the handoff.

With blockchain technology, DDOS (Distributed Denial of Service) attacks can be prevented since the chains/transactions are saved on multiple servers or computers making it hard for one to take down the entire chain when the attack targets a single location.

Blockchain technology can also help improve privacy. There are only a few public blockchains that anyone in the system can view. However, there is a serious option that can be used to ensure the privacy of more sensitive data and files such as electronic health records where only you, the health care professional and the insurance provider, are capable of accessing the information.

The blockchain is a distributed database which allows two parties to exchange data or information without the need for an intermediary. This way, risk can be eliminated or reduced thus making the blockchain data secure, consistent, timely, complete and widely available to individuals with proper authorization. Due to the decentralized nature of the blockchain, it is very resistant to malicious attacks. Any changes made to data on the blockchain can be viewed from any node in the blockchain, preventing the data from being deleted.

Despite the advantages, the blockchain is a new technology that faces a number of challenges. Due to its nascent state, the technology is unregulated, so government regulations will not have an impact on uptake and regularization of blockchain technology. The transactions in a blockchain also grow. The verification of these transactions can take a long time. In 2016, a single Bitcoin transaction took about 43 minutes to be verified. In the case of banking transactions such as ATM withdrawals, the transactions are processed almost instantly and updated in the financial ledger immediately. It is also possible to complete interbank transactions within a number of seconds. With the growth of transactions, the verification time may increase, and it could take longer to process even the small transactions. This is one of the current limitations of blockchain technology.

Blockchain applications provide solutions that provide significant changes to or even complete replacement of existing systems. For a transition to be made to blockchain technology, companies must plan for it so it can integrate well with existing systems and maximize savings in terms of transaction costs but with a high capital investment upfront.

Chapter 7- SHA-256

It is good for you to know how hashing is done in the blockchain. Hashing is the process of taking an input string of any length and producing a fixed-length output. In the blockchain technologies such as Bitcoin, the transactions are taken, then passed through a hashing algorithm which in turn gives a fixed-length output. Bitcoin uses the SHA-256 (Secure Hashing Algorithm) hashing algorithm.

In the SHA-256 hashing algorithm, no matter the length of the input string, the output has a fixed length of 256 bits. This is of great importance when you are dealing huge data or many transactions. This means that instead of having to remember the input string which might be large, you only have to remember and track the output.

A cryptographic has function as simply a special class of hashing algorithms with a number of properties that make them suitable and applicable in cryptography. A cryptographic hash function should be deterministic, meaning that no matter the number of times you pass a particular string through the hash function, you should always get the same output. This is very important because if you are unable to get similar output for same input, tracking the input may be difficult. The hash function should also provide quick computation so that the hash of an input string can be returned quickly. It should also be pre-image resistant; given a hash H(A), it is computationally unfeasible for you to get the string A that maps to the hash. If a small change is made on the input string, then the hash value should change greatly. This includes even a change in the case of one of the letters in the input string as this should produce a huge change in the hash value. A good hash function should be collision resistant, meaning that no two different strings can give the same hash value.

Blockchains heavily rely on the use of hashing algorithms. The data contained in the blockchain is hashed in each block. In case the data is changed, that is, someone changes the amount of Bitcoins they own or how much they owe someone else, the hash value will then be different and everyone in the blockchain will be able to detect this change.

The hashed value for a previous block is used to calculate the hashed value for the current block, creating a link between the two blocks. The use of the SHA-256 hashing algorithm makes mining of blocks difficult because the SHA-256 of a block's header should be equal 0 or lower than target for the block to be accepted into the network.

Let us explain this further. The hash of each block normally begins with a number of zeros. There is a very low probability of calculating a hash that begins with many zeros, meaning that the miner has to make many attempts. For the miner to be able to generate a new hash, he must increment the nonce.

Difficulty Adjustment

The difficulty is simply the measure of how difficult it is for one to find the new block compared to how easy it can be. It is recalculated for every 2016 blocks to a value in such a way that the previous 2016 blocks could have been mined in two weeks if everyone was mining this difficulty. This way, one block will be generated every 10 seconds.

As the number of miners on the blockchain increases, the rate at which blocks are created willalso go up. At the same time, the difficulty of block generation will go up so that the rate of generation is pushed down. There are malicious miners on the network. The blocks generated by such miners do not meet the required difficulty target, hence everyone on the network will reject them, making them worthless.

The network is responsible for automatically adjusting the difficulty of the mathematical problem, with the target being to solve six blocks every hour. The network comes to a consensus or agreement and the difficulty of mining blocks is increased or decreased based on the condition.

Chapter 8- Examples of Blockchains

There are various examples of blockchains. Let us discuss them:

Bitcoin Blockchain

Bitcoin is a new currency created by an unknown person going by the alias, Satoshi Nakamoto. The transactions are executed with no middlemen. One is not charged transaction fees and doesn't require a real name to use Bitcoin. Since it is a digital currency, it is held electronically. Bitcoins are not printed like euros and dollars, but they are produced by individuals and businesses, running computers all over the world using software to solve mathematical problems.

One can use Bitcoins to buy things electronically. However, the Bitcoin characteristic that makes it different from other currencies is that it is decentralized. No single individual or institution is tasked with the responsibility of controlling the Bitcoin network. The idea behind the development of Bitcoin was to come up with a currency which works without the control of a centralized authority. There was a need for a currency that can be transferred electronically while charging a very little transaction fee.

The production of Bitcoin is done by a community of people and anyone can join. The Bitcoins are mined in a distributed network by computing power. The network processes transactions made of the virtual currency, making Bitcoin its payment network.

People use software programs to produce Bitcoins. Bitcoin balances are stored using private and public keys that are long strings of letters and numbers generated using algorithms. The public key serves as the address publicized to the world and people may send Bitcoins to it. The private key should be kept as a secret and only used for the purpose of authorizing transactions.

The Bitcoin was one of the first digital currencies of the world to use a peer-to-peer technology for the purpose of facilitating instant payments. The individuals and companies that take part in the Bitcoin network and possess computing power are motivated through rewards and transaction fees paid in Bitcoins. They are known as "miners". The miners can be seen as a decentralized authority responsible for enforcing the credibility of the network. The Bitcoin generation process is controlled so that they don't exceed 21 million Bitcoins. This is a good way of controlling inflation. Each Bitcoin can be divided into eight decimal places, and the smallest unit is given the name Satoshi. If it is necessary and the miners agree, it is possible for the Bitcoin to be made divisible into more decimal places.

Bitcoin mining is the process through which the Bitcoins are released into circulation. The process involves solving some difficult mathematical problems in a bid to discover a new block, which is in turn is added to the blockchain. The miners earn rewards in the form of Bitcoins. As more and more Bitcoins are mined and added to the blockchain, the difficulty or the computing power needed to mine Bitcoins increases. During the early days of Bitcoin, a normal computer was enough for mining Bitcoins. However, with the increase in the difficulty of mining Bitcoins, miners use more specific hardware tools such as the Application-Specific Integrated Circuits (ASIC) and more powerful processing units such as the Graphical Process Unit (GPU).

Most Bitcoin users believe that it will form the future currency because Bitcoin facilitates a faster and non-fee payment method for sending transactions all over the world. Although Bitcoin is not backed by any government or even a central bank, it can be exchanged with traditional currency, with its good exchange rate with the US dollar attracting traders and investors interested in currency plays. One of the reasons behind the growth of digital currencies such as Bitcoin is they can be used as an alternative to traditional commodities such as gold and national fiat money.

You can easily obtain Bitcoins in the same way that you get other currencies. You can sell something you own and get paid through Bitcoins. You can also ask your employer to pay your salary in the form of Bitcoins. There are also many online exchanges from where you can buy Bitcoins.

Ethereum Blockchain

Other than Bitcoin, there are several other applications of the blockchain technology that go beyond digital currencies. Ethereum is simply an open software platform that provides software developers with a platform where they can build decentralized applications. The applications can also be deployed there. Just like Bitcoin, Ethereum is a distributed and public blockchain network. The two have significant technical capabilities, but they also differ greatly in terms of purpose and capability. The Bitcoin is more concerned with ownership of digital currency, while Ethereum is more focused on writing programming code for any decentralized application.

The goal of Bitcoin is to disrupt online banking and PayPal, but the goal of Ethereum is to use the blockchain to disrupt Internet third parties, those responsible for storing data, transferring mortgages and keeping track of complex financial instruments.

To make it simpler, the goal of Ethereum is to be a "world computer" that will decentralize the client-server model. In the Ethereum blockchain, clouds and servers are replaced by thousands of "nodes" run by volunteers from all over the globe to form a "world computer". The vision is Ethereum will allow this to be available to all people across the globe and enable them to compete to offer services on top of the infrastructure.

A good example is when you visit an app store. You will find a wide variety of apps including messaging, banking and fitness. The apps depend on the company or a third party to store information related to your credit cards, purchasing history and personal data, held somewhere in servers controlled by third parties. The apps you choose will also be determined by third parties such as Google and Apple who curate the specific ones you are able to download.

With Ethereum, if all goes as planned, the control of data in these types of services will return to the owner and the creative rights to the author. The goal is that no single entity will have control over your notes and no one can ban the app itself, temporarily taking all notes offline. Only the user is able to make changes, but not any other entity.

Theoretically, Ethereum combines the control that people exercised over their information in the past with the ease of access to information that most people are used to in the digital age. Every time you save edits, add or even delete some notes, each node running in the network is updated.

Note that in the Ethereum blockchain, instead of miners mining for Bitcoin, they have to work to earn ether. Ether is the crypto token that fuels the network. Other than being used as a tradable cryptocurrency, ether is used to pay application developers for transaction fees and services on the Ethereum network.

A smart contract is simply a computer code that facilitates the exchange of money, property, content, shares or anything with value. When a smart contract is running on the blockchain, it becomes like a computer program that runs automatically after certain conditions are met. Since the smart contracts run on the blockchain, they simply run as they have been programmed without the possibility of censorship, fraud, downtime or third party interference.

Although all blockchains are capable of processing code, most are limited. However, Ethereum is different. Instead of giving some set of limited operations, Ethereum normally allows its developers to create any operations they need. This is an indication that the developers are capable of developing a wide variety of applications beyond what we have been able to see.

Before the development of Ethereum, blockchain applications could only be used for performing a limited set of operations. Bitcoin and the other few cryptocurrencies were, for example, designed and developed to be used as peer-to-peer digital currencies. However, they developed a number of challenges. They had to expand the set of functionalities supported by Bitcoin, a complex and time-consuming process, or develop a completely new blockchain.

The core innovation of Ethereum is the Ethereum Virtual Machine (EVM) which is a Turing complete software that runs on the Ethereum network. It allows anyone to run programs, regardless of the programming language used when provided with enough time and memory. The EVM has made the process of creating blockchain applications easier than before. Instead of developers having to create a completely new blockchain for every application, Ethereum provides developers with a single platform where they can develop their applications.

With Ethereum, we are able to develop and deploy decentralized applications. A decentralized application (Dapp) is developed and provided to users for a particular purpose. Bitcoin is an example of a Dapp providing a peer-to-peer electronic cash system enabling users to make online Bitcoin payments. Since the decentralized applications have code that runs on the blockchain network, no single individual or centralized authority controls them.

Ethereum can help to decentralize any centralized service. Consider the intermediary service provided in many industries such as the loans offered by banks and the services offered by voting systems, title registries, regulatory compliance and several others.

Ethereum can also be used to build Decentralized Autonomous Organizations (DAO). This is simply a fully decentralized and autonomous organization with no single leader. A DAO is simply run by computer programming code on many Ethereum contracts written on the Ethereum blockchain. The code is normally designed in such a way that it replaces the rules and structure of the traditional organization, doing away with people and the need for centralized control. Anyone who purchases tokens owns the DAO, but instead of each token being equal to equity shares and ownership, the tokens are used as contributions giving people voting rights.

Despite the many advantages associated with decentralized applications, they are also associated with a number of faults. The smart contracts running on the blockchain are written by humans, meaning that they are only as good as they have been written. Bugs in the code can lead to inappropriate actions. Mistakes in the code can also be exploited, and there is no way of rectifying the mistake other than getting a network consensus and rewriting the whole code. However, the essence of the blockchain is to be immutable, and doing so will go against this principle.

Ripple Blockchain

Ripple refers to both a digital currency (XRP) and an open payment network through which the currency is transferred. It is an open-source, distributed payment system that is still in beta. The essence of the ripple system is to enable people to break free of the "walled gardens" of financial networks, that is, banks, credit cards, PayPal and other institutions that normally restrict access by charging fees, processing delays and charging for currency exchanges.

The Ripple blockchain was developed to address the need to keep money flowing freely. Banks and other financial institutions restricts the transfer of money by charging fees and other means. Ripple is built on the decentralized digital currency approach set by Bitcoin that use the Internet to do for money what it did for all other types of information. In the case of payment systems providers, each provider builds his own system for customers. Ripple was developed to connect different payment systems together.

OpenCoin is the company behind the development of Ripple. CEO, Chris Larsen, and CTO, Jed McCaleb, are the co-founders of OpenCoin. McCaleb had good knowledge of digital currency since he came from Mt. Gox, the company that does most of the world's Bitcoin trades. The other developers in the Ripple's team also had a Bitcoin background.

Ripple and Bitcoin are closely related. The Ripple's XRP unit is simply a digital form of currency based on mathematical formulae with a limited number of units we can mine. The currency can also be transferred from one account to another without the need for any third party intervention. Both Bitcoin and XRP provide a form of digital security as a way of guarding against the possibility of counterfeit coins.

You may think that Ripple is a competitor of Bitcoin, but this is not the case. Instead, Ripple acts as a complement to Bitcoin. The Ripple network was designed and built to allow for a seamless transfer of various forms of currency, including euros, dollars, pounds, Bitcoins, yen, etc. It opens up many gateways for Bitcoin users and provides them with easy ways to bridge Bitcoin and the world of finance.

Other than providing Bitcoin with ways to connect using other types of currency, it promises increased stability and expedited transactions. Since Ripple is a distributed network, there is no need for relying on a single company to secure and manage the transaction database. Also, there is no need to wait for block confirmations, and confirmations of transactions can quickly go through the network. Due to the use of peer-to-peer, the system does not have a central point of failure.

The Ripple system does not collect fees in the same way as banks, PayPal and credit card institutions. However, it takes a small amount of ripple from each transaction. The amount is destroyed instead of kept. This deduction helps to protect the system against being swamped by individuals who may try to run too many transactions at once.

Chapter 9- Applications of Blockchain

Blockchain technology has revolutionized recording systems. Since the invention of Bitcoin, industries from all over the world know the implications of its development. Blockchain technology has brought about vast creativity across the world since it can be applied anywhere there is a need for a trustworthy record. It also puts the full power of cryptography in the hands of individuals, stopping digital transactions from needing a transaction authority to "pull transactions".

Let us discuss the various applications of the Blockchain technology:

Secure Smart Contracts

The blockchain provides the crating and securing of digital relationships. A group of the largest banks in the world and insurance companies is looking for ways to build a platform through which digital relationships between banks will be established. These new digital relationships will be secured by combining coded business logic and Ricardian contracts.

This version of smart contracts is looking for ways to use documents and information kept in the blockchains to support complex legal agreements. There are also startups working on sidechains, or bespoke blockchains plugged into the larger public blockchains. These "federated blockchains" are capable of overcoming problems such as the block size debate plaguing Bitcoin. It is expected that these groups will create blockchains that authorize some super-specific types of transactions.

With Ethereum, this idea is taken further. A new kind of smart contract has been introduced, whose vision to apply business logic on the blockchain to be able to code transactions of any kind, then authorize them when the network runs the code.

The primary purpose of Ethereum is to become a platform for smart contract code, made up of programs controlling blockchain assets, executed by the blockchain protocol, and in our case, running on the Ethereum network. The purpose of having an intermediary for any transaction is to ensure that the parties follow the necessary terms. The blockchain does away with the need for third parties and ensures that all individuals participating in the ledger know the details of the contract and that the terms of the contract implement automatically once the conditions are met.

Smart contracts can be used for all types of situations, including insurance premiums, financial derivatives, crowd funding agreements, property law and several others. An example of a blockchain smart contract is blockchain healthcare. Personal health records can be encoded then stored on the blockchain using a private key so that only specific individuals will be granted access. This strategy can also be employed to ensure that research is done according to specified laws such as HIPAA laws. Surgery receipts can be kept on the blockchain then send tto an insurance provider as a proof-of-delivery. The ledger may also be used for a general health care management like regulation compliance, supervising drugs, managing healthcare supplies and testing results.

Blockchain music is another example of a blockchain smart contract. Some of the problems facing the music industry include royalty distribution, ownership rights and transparency. The digital music industry normally focusses on the monetization of productions, but the ownership rights are overlooked. The smart contract technology of the blockchain can be used to create an accurate and comprehensive decentralized database for music rights. This will provide a transparent way of transferring artists' royalties and a real-time distribution to all those involved with labels.

Secure Anonymous Transactions

Most individuals, hackers and businesses have expressed interest in cryptocurrencies. One of the factors contributing to the popularity of Bitcoin is anonymity. However, concerns have been raised that online transactions will not be as anonymous as people hope.

In cryptocurrencies, encryption techniques are used to regulate the generation of currency units and verification of transfer of funds; and this is done without the involvement of the central bank. It is a trustless, decentralized money system that may be verified independently of any central authority. This is done using the blockchain, which is a list of open and encrypted records. Bitcoin is the father of all cryptocurrencies, and it requires a record of transactions or a ledger made available to anyone. This leads to anonymity and privacy concerns. However, this issue has been addressed.

Since the blockchain ledger is public, it becomes hard to ensure that there be anonymity. Bitcoin is considered as pseudoanonymous, meaning that an individual may be linked to a public Bitcoin address, but not the actual home address or name. You are able to know that a particular address is associated with an individual but you can't know who that individual is. This makes it the best currency for carrying out transactions in which you need to remain anonymous. This is why hackers ask for payments through Bitcoins. Other groups that prefer Bitcoins for the level of anonymity they offer include drug traffickers and gun smugglers. There are various reasons why people like to be anonymous when carrying out transactions online. They include company-specific information, law-enforcement issues and for the purpose of maintaining privacy. Hackers are mostly using cryptocurrencies for carrying out their financial transactions. Well-known underground markets selling malware, stolen-personal data as well as other goods and services, transact using cryptocurrencies.

Blockchain users are not encouraged to give out personally-identifiable information. Users should not link their personal or company information to a transaction or cryptocurrency address. A website possesses personal data such as registrar information and an IP address. These two must be addressed when used in relation to the service or site. For one to stay anonymous, it is recommended they buy Bitcoins in the form of cash.

Anonymity is based on trust of the organization or the person with whom you trade and how securely they store information. Blockchain technology is a good way of transacting anonymously.

How to Profit from Blockchain Technologies

The blockchain provides various technologies from which we can benefit. There are various ways to make money. Big international corporations are jumping into this new technology. The question is, how can you join them and profit yourself?

1. Mining

You can make the blockchain a bank by mining cryptocurrencies. In the blockchain, a block is made up of multiple transactions. The miners go through a process to verify the blocks. A block is passed through a mathematical formula or algorithm so as to give a "hash". The hash is simply a sequence of alphanumeric characters.

During the creation of the hash for a block, the hash of the previous block is used. After sealing off a block, a lot of activity normally happens. The first miner to generate the hash is rewarded. This will vary from one cryptocurrency to another. Currently, Bitcoin has a reward of 12 Bitcoins. As more of the mining takes place, the reward is halved.

When Bitcoin was first introduced into the market, there were very few miners. However, people realized that there is much potential in mining cryptocurrency and many joined the network. During these early days, a CPU or a GPU alone was enough for Bitcoin mining.

The increase in the number of miners has led to the pop up of mining pools. These are individuals who team up to mine the Bitcoins by combining their computing power and resources. This way, there is a high probability that the team will complete the hash.

Once the pool wins, every member of the pool is given a portion of the reward.

2. Trading

Just like fiat money, you can find cryptocurrencies in the exchanges. However, they are closely related to stocks as compared to other types of exchanges. Due to the high volatility of cryptocurrency markets, one can see it as a risk to invest in them.

However, trading cryptocurrencies is similar to penny stock trading. Penny stocks fluctuate greatly. However, after doing research, it can be easy for you to trade in them. There are thousands of cryptocurrencies that you can trade.

However, you must be updated about everything to do with cryptocurrency frequently. Do your research and read the market. You will then make money from the blockchain.

3. Stockpiling Bitcoin

In the same way that investors stockpile gold, you can stockpile Bitcoins and profit from it. Gold is tangible while Bitcoin is intangible, but the investment principles in both cases are similar. Also, the two are considered to be rare. Initially, Bitcoins were generated at a higher rate compared to the rate at which they are generated today. This is because the market is almost hitting the target of 21 million Bitcoins.

When stockpiling Bitcoins, follow the basic principle of supply and demand. When the supply is limited, the demand increases, and the value also rises. There are many ways to acquire or purchase Bitcoins, so stockpiling can be an easy task for you.

4. Altcoin Crowdfunding

Crowdfunding is now considered to be one of the many ways to raise seed capital in various types of investments. If you need to take part in the blockchain technology, consider a crowdfunding method using alternative coins. The total coin supply is pre-mined then sold in an initial coin offering (ICO) prior to the network being launched publicly. Bitshares are an example of the various coin networks that used this method when getting started. Applications and services that use blockchain technology have also used this method to raise funds. This gives investors an opportunity to purchase coins while expecting that their prices will increase at some point in the future in case the service becomes popular.

5. Angel Funding and Startup Ventures

Angel funding and investing in startups is not a new concept. One of the variations that is beginning to gain traction is investing in startups built on blockchain technology The popularity of Bitcoin has increased and most businesses have accepted it. Due to this, there are many entrepreneurs willing to practice with the technology behind this cryptocurrency. Such a startup will need some funding. However, note that while the profits from such an investment are massive, the risks are high.

6. Pure Blockchain Technology Play

   Currently, there are several pure blockchain technology plays. Companies like BTCS, hashing Space Corporation, Global Area Holding and Inc. are becoming very popular in the industry. A company such as BTCS works to secure the blockchain through its distinctive transaction verification services. Global Arena Holding is working to leverage blockchain technology to use in voting verification.

You can weigh all the above methods of investing in blockchain technology and choose the method that puts you at the lowest risk. If you need to keep your risk low, invest in stocks provided by one of the largest financial services currently experimenting with blockchain technology to determine its potential for improving services. If you are ready to tolerate a higher degree of risk and in turn get a huge return, you can choose to invest in one of the pure blockchain investment opportunities and you end up with a good combination of risk vs. returns.

There are numerous opportunities associated with blockchain, and the technology is more promising. Tap into this technology and you will enjoy the profits.

Blockchain for Finance and Industry

Blockchain technology can help to revolutionize the finance industry. Its proponents believe that it can be used to create secure and convenient alternatives to expensive and time-consuming bank processes. It is gaining much traction since each bank in the world is trying to implement the use of this technology.

For example, banks are creating systems that reduce the numbers of users participating in a transaction. However, some banks have invested more heavily in this than others. Others are investing in the blockchain startups. Others have partnered with fintech companies that make use of blockchain.

The global financial industries serves billions of people each day and trillions of dollars are transacted. However, the system is full of problems including fees for costs and delays, creating opportunities for crime and fraud and giving rise to friction through onerous and redundant paperwork. 45% of all intermediaries taking part in financial transactions including stock exchanges, payment networks and money transfer services experience an economic crime each year. This is why regulatory costs for banks are increasing each day and it is fast becoming an issue of concern. It adds extra costs, and consumers have to bear the burden.

The question is, what makes the financial system so inefficient? The first reason is that it is antiquated, a paper-based process and industrial technologies dressed up in a digital wrapper. Secondly, the system is centralized, making it resistant to change and more prone to system attacks and failures. Thirdly, the system denies billions of people access to basic financial tools. The only solution to these problems is blockchain technology.

The blockchain was developed as the technology underlying cryptocurrencies such as Bitcoin. However, since it is simply a distributed ledger, it is capable of recording anything that has value. Assets such as money, bonds, equities, titles, contracts, deeds and other instruments can be moved and stored privately, securely and from peer to peer, since trust is not established through governments and banks, but through network consensus, collaboration, cryptography and clever code. It is through Bitcoin that two parties, businesses or individuals, are able to enter into agreements, build transactions and create value without the need for intermediaries to establish trust, verify their identities or perform the critical business logic like clearing, contracting and record-keeping that are very essential in commerce.

Given all these advantages, many financial institutions like banks are venturing into this technology. Most of these institutions cite the need to reduce costs and frictions as the reason behind investing in the technology.

Banks are encouraged to use blockchain-based systems to circumvent legacy infrastructure or central bodies. The banks can develop such systems to come up with new business models capable of disrupting the financial ecosystem. Fintechs are also using blockchain technologies to provide their services like international payments and remittances with greater speed at a reduced cost and with user-friendly interfaces than the banks.

With blockchain, financial institutions are able to access up-to-date, trusted attribute information about customers and improve the accuracy of the know-your-customer (KYC) process. With blockchain, real time point-to-point transfer of funds between financial institutions can be done, removing frictions and accelerating settlements. Blockchain technology also brings about increased trust and visibility across participants and helps in reducing delays, manual effort and costs with smart contracts. These shows that the blockchain technology is very beneficial to the financial industry. Financial institutions are encouraged to invest in this technology that promises to revolutionize the sector.

Blockchains for Securing Business Transactions

Hackers around the world are trying to hack into banking systems and other financial institutions and transfer money into their own accounts. In blockchain technology, another obstacle stands in the way to prevent this. Even if a hacker gains illegal access to the network and tries to steal funds, there are multiple copies of the same ledger stored all over the world. In case the hacker tampers with one of them, the other ledgers will help in verifying the transactions and identify the funds belonging to which account.

However, just like with all digital systems, there might be a weak point yet to be known; but with the current banking and financial technology infrastructure, the flaws may be secured, patched and upgraded to ensure the financial transactions are as secure as intended.

Cryptography is used to secure the records in a blockchain transaction, and each transaction is linked to the previous one to form a chain. The transaction records are distributed and can be viewed by each ledger participant. For the hacker to succeed in changing the transaction, he will also have to change all the previous records in the blockchain.

In addition, blockchain transactions are validated by the algorithms on the nodes, that is, the computers on the network of participants in a distributed ledger. It is impossible for a single entity to create a transaction. Also, with blockchain, transparency is enhanced, and each participant is given the ability to monitor the transactions at any time they need to do so.

The participants are capable of setting up either a private or a public blockchain. With a private blockchain, the number of trusted and verified participants is limited. Other than cracking the cryptology, the blockchain can be seen as one of the most secure digital capabilities in the world. This is why private blockchains are highly used in financial contexts. The participants are able to control who accesses the ledger of verified transactions, the one capable of submitting transactions and the one who can verify them.

Before creating a private blockchain, you must consider the architecture of the underlying network infrastructure as this is where the security begins. For the participants to come to a consensus, communication is needed. Communication is also needed for new transactions to be written and approved. This communication is done between nodes, with each maintaining a copy of the ledger and informing the rest on any new information. With a private blockchain, the operators are able to control who operates a node, as well as how the connections between the nodes can be done. A node with more connection will receive information faster. Also, the nodes may be required to maintain a particular number of connections to be considered as active. Any node that transmits incorrect information or restricts the transfer of information would be identified then circumvented to maintain the integrity of the entire system.

For security purposes in the network infrastructure, a proper way of handling intermitted or uncommunicative active nodes should be established. There are various reasons why nodes can go offline, but it is good for the network to be structured to ensure that it functions without offline nodes; and the network should be in a position to bring up the nodes faster whenever they go offline.

Chapter 10- Hands on - How you can you use Bitcoin

Create Wallet

In a blockchain such as Bitcoin, one of the safest ways of keeping your coins is through a wallet. A Bitcoin wallet is made up of two keys. You will be more familiar with the public key, the wallet address used by other people to send Bitcoins to you. The other part of the Bitcoin wallet is the private key. This helps you send Bitcoins to other people. When the public key of the recipient and your private key are combined, cryptocurrency transactions are possible. Note that if anyone grabs your private key, it would be possible for them to withdraw your funds; thus you should not disclose this key to anyone.

You may choose to keep your coins in an online wallet or a hard-drive-based software wallet; but in all cases, you will be vulnerable to attacks by hackers or any malware capable of capturing your keystrokes. You can visit **BlockChain.info** to begin creating a wallet for your coins. You can then follow the steps below to create the wallet:

1. On the top menu, click the "Wallet" button
2. Click the "Create a new wallet" button.
3. Enter your e-mail address and your password, then confirm your password.
4. Click the "Continue" button.
   You can write down, take a screenshot or print your mnemonic password. This will help you recover your password in case you lose it.
   Click "Continue".
5. Type in your password, then click the "Open Wallet" button. Ensure that you have written down your identifier.

Your Bitcoin address will be printed at the bottom of the screen presented to you.

A paper wallet refers to a document with copies of private and public keys that make up your wallet. This will have the QR codes, so these can be scanned and added into a software wallet to carry out a transaction. A paper wallet has a benefit in that the keys are not stored digitally in any place, meaning that they are not subject to hardware failures or cyber-attacks. However, it has a disadvantage in that paper and ink may degrade and paper is fragile, meaning that you have to keep it away from water and fire. Also, in case you lose the paper wallet, you will not be able to access the Bitcoins sent to the address.

To create a paper wallet, follow these steps:

1. Open your browser, then open the **BitAddress.org** address. For LiteCoin, you can open **LiteAddress.org**.

2. In the case of BitAddress, you will be asked to create randomness simply by typing some random characters into a form or by moving the cursor around randomly.

3. You will be shown your public and private keys as well as their QR codes. Don't scan them.

4. Click the tab for "Paper wallet".

5. Choose the number of addresses you need to generate.

6. If you don't need to keep the Bitcoin artwork, click the "Hide art?" button.

7. Click the button for "Generate" to create new wallets.

8. After the wallets have been generated, you can click the "Print" button so that you can make a hard copy of them.

9. The browser will prompt you to choose the printer you need to use. If you are using Google Chrome as the browser, you will be able to print the file as a PDF.

10. Write down the public addresses, or scan the QR code for the public address in the Bitcoin app, then begin to deposit the funds.

On the Blockchain.info website, there is also an option for a basic paper wallet. You can click on the "Import/Export" option, then look for the "Paper wallet" link located on the left-hand menu.

Generating a Bitcoin Vanity Address

A Bitcoin vanity address is a Bitcoin address that uses characters that are appealing to you. It is similar to having a personalized license plate for your car. The vanity address is optional, but it is a good way of seeing your message in Bitcoin. You can use BitcoinVanityGen.com to generate a Bitcoin vanity address. The following steps can help:

1. On your browser, open the **BitcoinVanityGen.com** website.
2. In the field for Type Letters, enter your six letters. Note that only small messages are allowed in Bitcoin and the vanity address will make the content for your message. These can be easily read in Bitcoin. It is recommended that you choose something cool since you will be allowed to reuse the address whenever you want after it has been created.
3. Click Generate. Click Email.
4. Type in your email address.

Once the vanity has been found, the BitcoinVanityGen.com will email it to you.

5. Open the email message you receive from BitcoinVanityGen.com, then click the link you find in the message. You will be given the vanity address as well as the private key associated with it.

6. Copy the address and the private key, then keep them in a safe place. The address and private key will be needed later, so copy them.

If you don't need to generate the address yourself, you can outsource the work from Bitcoin vanity address miners. The miners will dedicate their GPU and CPU power to finding the Bitcoin the address you need and will send it to you via email. However, this is risky in that the miners may choose to hold the private key that has generated the vanity address, then use it to steal the coin you store in the generated vanity address. This is why you should use the above discussed mechanism to generate the vanity address on your own and stay safe.

Transferring a Vanity Address

After a blockchain vanity address has been generated, you will need to transfer it to your wallet. This will allow you to manage your address as well as send and receive Bitcoins more easily. The following steps can help you do the transfer:

1. Log into your **Blockchain.info wallet.**
2. Click on Settings, then click on Addresses.
3. Click "Manage Addresses" located next to "Imported Addresses".
4. Click on "Import Addresses", type in your private key, then click "Import". You will have created an address that will allow you to read your vanity address when sending or receiving Bitcoins.

How to Buy Bitcoins

Bitcoins can be bought from either exchanges or from other people directly via marketplaces. There are also various ways that you can pay for the Bitcoins, ranging from the use of hard cash to credit and debit cards, wire transfers, and even buying them using other cryptocurrencies depending on where you are buying them and where you are located.

Note that buying Bitcoins through PayPal or credit cards is still not easy. This is because such transactions can easily be reversed through a phone call to the credit card company. In the transfer of Bitcoins, it is hard for one to prove that an exchange of goods took place, and this is why these payment methods are to be avoided. However, these payment methods have grown in usage in some countries.

In the US, for example, Circle and Coinbase offer payment through credit cards. CoinCorner, Bittylicious and Coinbase also offer this service in the UK, accepting 3D secure-enabled debit and credit cards on MasterCard and Visa networks. Underbanked US consumers can use Expresscoin, launched recently for the purpose of serving this market by accepting personal checks, money orders and wire transfers.

Got a Bitooin Wallet

You should have a place where you can store your Bitcoins after purchasing them. This is a "wallet", but it is good to think of it as a bank account. We have already discussed the process of getting a Bitcoin wallet, so if you don't have one, go through those steps to get one. Various types of wallets provide different levels of security. Some offer basic security, while others offer military-grade protection.

As a newcomer to Bitcoin, you may experience a challenge in choosing the best exchange for your business. Some of these exchanges offer a wide range of services, while others provide the simple capabilities of buying and selling Bitcoins. Most exchanges and wallets can store both digital and fiat currencies for you, while others store only one of these. If you want to take part in regular trades and speculation, exchanges and wallets are the best options for you. They don't require full anonymity, and they provide their users with simple setup steps.

Over-the-counter (OTC) or Face-to-face Trades

If you prefer anonymity, you live in a city, or you don't need bank hassles, the best way for you to acquire Bitcoins is by making a face-to-face trade with a local Bitcoin seller.

LocalBitcoins forms the primary site where you can arrange for such transactions and negotiate the prices. Escrow services are offered as a way of protecting both parties. However, you must be cautious when engaging in these types of trades. Ensure that you meet the trader in a public place, but avoid private places for security reasons. Also, be wary when carrying huge amounts of money.

If you are to meet somewhere with the Bitcoin seller, you must have access to your wallet. You should have a laptop, smartphone or tablet and Internet access.

If you are not interested in a one-on-one trade, check out **Meetout.com** and see whether there is a Bitcoin meetup group in your area. You will be able to purchase Bitcoins from this group and learn a lot.

An Investment Trust

If you are not interested in buying and storing large amounts of Bitcoins, you can choose an investment trust like the Winklevoss ETF or Bitcoin Investment Trust (BIT). These use a state-of-the-art protocol to store Bitcoins on your behalf. The Bitcoin Superfund is another option for those living in the UK.

Bitcoin ATMs

This is a new concept with increasing popularity. Examples of Bitcoin ATM vendors include CoinOutlet, BitAccess, Genesis Coin, Robocoin and Lamassu. It is like the face-to-face mechanism but a machine is involved in this case. You insert cash, then you either scan your mobile wallet QR code or get a paper receipt with the codes necessary to load the Bitcoins into the wallet.

The exchange rates vary, ranging between 3% and 8% on top of a standard exchange fee. You should stay updated with the latest Bitcoin ATM news.

Exchanges and Online Wallets

There are various exchanges and online wallets competing with each other. Some of the exchanges are full-blown and good for institutional traders, while others are simple wallet services providing a limited buying and selling capability. Most wallets and exchanges work like regular bank accounts by storing both by storing digital or/and fiat currency for you.

Wallets and exchanges are the best option if need to engage in regular trading and speculation; you don't need total anonymity and you don't incur any lengthy or bureaucratic procedures that involve supplying detailed contact information and proof of identity.

Mining

Most people have heard about mining Bitcoins using the own PC or a graphics processing unit (GPU). This was possible in the early days of Bitcoin, but more powerful Bitcoin tools have since been introduced. This has also increased the difficulty and energy required for one to mine a worthwhile amount of Bitcoins. Remember, the number of Bitcoin remaining for mining reduces sharply with time because many people are venturing into Bitcoin mining. This means that it is not effective for one to mine Bitcoins as an individual. Doing so can result in spending more on hardware and electricity than you are earning Bitcoins in return.

Nowadays, Bitcoin mining is done in groups known as "pools" and by companies that have been setup specifically for mining. It is recommended that you buy shares from such a company or pool. You can also choose to join "cloud mining", where instead of investing in fast-dating and expensive equipment, you pay to use the data centers of a particular company and mine on their behalf. The best way to earn Bitcoins through mining is by joining a Bitcoin mining pool. This way, you will combine your mining skills and resources and earn rewards in the form of Bitcoins.

How to Buy Something with Bitcoins

When one looks at Bitcoin as an alternative currency, the question is, where can one spend Bitcoin? The answer is that it can be used anywhere, including for shopping and paying for groceries in a local supermarket. There are various e-commerce websites that accept Bitcoins in exchange for goods and services. Many bricks-and-mortar stores are now accepting cryptocurrency as a form of payment.

The best way to look for Bitcoin-accepting merchants is through marketplaces and aggregator sites that gather huge numbers of supporting establishments together at once. With CoinMap.org, one is provided with a visual way to locate Bitcoin stores in any area.

Microsoft has added Bitcoin as a form of payment for various digital content across its platform. US-based customers are now able to add money to their accounts, and they can use this money to purchase content such as games, apps and videos from Windows, Xbox and Windows phone platforms.

Bitcoin Gift Cards

If you are unable to find online or physical stores that accept Bitcoin for the items you need, then gift cards are the easiest way to turn your Bitcoins into real goods and services. Most gift card businesses accept Bitcoins and these cards can be used on various retailers such as Amazon, Walmart, Nike and Target. For the case of US customers, companies such as eGifter, Gyft, GiftCardZen and iTradeBTC have a wide range of options.

For UK customers, Gift Off will allow you to use 15 cryptocurrencies to buy gift cards for 177 retailers like Ryan Air, Amazon, American Apparel and Mark & Spencer. This service is expected to be introduced to the EU, with Germany and France to receive various gift card options.

It is good to note that the majority of gift cards only remain valid in their country of issue, which in most cases is the United States. One also pays a little more in order to trade Bitcoins for gift cards, but there is no need to deal with transfers or exchanges.

Making Bitcoin Payments

It is fast, secure and convenient for one to make a Bitcoin payment. To make the payment, you are not expected to provide or enter any sensitive information. You simply have to send the payment from your wallet app, which can be done using any of the following three methods:

1. Scan the QR Code

   If your wallet is running on a different mobile device, you can scan the code to open the payment in the wallet. You will be allowed to confirm whether everything is correct, and the payment will be made.

2. Open in Wallet

   If your wallet is running on the device you are using to view the invoice, you can open the payment in the wallet by tapping. You will be allowed to confirm whether everything is correct, then make the payment.

3. Send the payment manually

   If your wallet doesn't support the above two methods, or in case you are using an older wallet, it is possible to send the payment manually. You should copy the address carefully and the correct Bitcoin amount from your invoice to the wallet, then send the payment manually.

Refunds & Order Troubleshooting

With BitPay, merchants are provided with tools and reporting to view successful payments and manage their own refunds in Bitcoin. If you want a refund or need some help regarding getting the order for a successful payment, you should directly contact the merchant. They can initiate the refund process or help you in getting a purchase.

Note that for the merchant to be able to assist you, you will have to provide your BitPay invoice URL or the order ID. Refund policies vary from merchant to merchant, so it is good to discuss the options with your merchant.

Use Smart Contracts with Bitcoins

The purpose of smart contracts is to help you exchange money shares, property or anything else of value in a conflict-free and transparent way while avoiding the need for a middleman. This technology can be compared to a vending machine. You would go to a notary or a lawyer, pay them, then you wait for the document. With a smart contract, you only have to drop the Bitcoin in a vending machine, that is, the ledger, and your escrow, driver's license or anything drops in your account. Note that some contracts do not only define the rules and penalties surrounding an agreement in the same way as a traditional one, but they also enforce these obligations automatically.

You can see smart contracts as a digitized form of traditional contracts. They are computer programs that run on the Blockchain database. One can program them so that they can be executed automatically once the conditions written in their source code are met. Users trust smart contracts due to the fact that once programmed, the conditions in them can't be changed, meaning they are immutable.

Smart contracts are written in a language known as Solidity, and they have numerous advantages when compared to traditional contracts. There is no need for a third party for the contract to be enforced. The terms of the contract are unchangeable, meaning that there are no chances of the users being cheated.

The work of writing a smart contract is done by developers. The written smart contract can be used for the transaction or the exchange of anything between two or more parties. Conditions are implemented within the code, and these must be met for the contract to self-execute.

After the smart contract code has been written, it is uploaded to the Blockchain network, that is, the code is sent to all the devices connected to the network. This is done in the same way that a network update regarding a Bitcoin transaction is uploaded to the Blockchain.

After the code has been uploaded to all devices, they must come to an agreement once the code has been executed. Once it is reached, the database is updated to record the execution of the code and check the terms of the contract to see whether they have been adhered to. This way, no single party can manipulate the contract since the control of the execution of the contract is not under the control of a single party.

Blockchain technology is now being integrated into most aspects of human life. Smart contracts are becoming a very critical part of the blockchain technology. The blockchain and smart contracts have many ramifications and use cases that have not yet been explored, but big companies are heavily investing into research.

Chapter 11- Limitations & Challenges of Blockchain Technology

Blockchain technology is in its early days of development, hence it is associated with a number of limitations that have made the technology inappropriate for a number of digital operations. The following are some of the challenges of blockchain technology:

1. Complexity

    Blockchain technology consists of completely new vocabulary. The technology has made cryptography more mainstream, and the industry is full of jargon. However, there is a rising emergence of indexes and glossaries that are easy to understand.

2. Network Size

    Just like all the other distributed systems, blockchains are not very resistant to bad actors due to their anti-fragile nature, that is, they normally respond to attacks and grow stronger. A large network of users is required. However, if the blockchain is not a robust network with a widely distributed grid of nodes, it becomes hard for you to enjoy its full benefits.

3. Transaction costs and network speed
   Initially, Bitcoin was known to be "near free" but it now has some transaction costs. The Bitcoin network is only capable of processing 7 transactions each second, with each transaction costing about $0.20 and only capable of storing 80 bytes of data. The use of the Bitcoins is also politically charged, not in terms of carrying out transactions, but in terms of storing information. The question of "bloating" is normally frowned upon since it forces miners to perpetually reprocess and record information.

4. Unavoidable security flaw
   Bitcoins and other blockchains have a security flaw, that is, if half the computers running on the blockchain tell a lie, then the lie will be treated as the truth. This is referred to as the "51% attack" and it was discovered by Satoshi Nakamoto when he launched the Bitcoin blockchain.

5. Politics
   The blockchain protocols provide an opportunity to digitize the governance models, and due to the fact

that the miners are forming a new type of incentivized governance model, it has provided a new opportunity for public disagreements between those running the different community sectors. These disagreements are very common in the blockchain industry and they are expressed around the question or event of "forking" a blockchain, a process involving updating a blockchain protocol when the majority of blockchain users have agreed on it. The debates are very technical, and they can sometimes be heated, but they are very informative to those interested in a mixture of consensus, democracy and new opportunities for governance experimentation opened by blockchain technology.

6. Human Error

If the blockchain is being used as a database, the information being added to the database should be of high quality. The data stored in the blockchain is not very trustworthy, so there is a need for events to be record accurately first. The "garbage in, garbage out" concept holds true in blockchain technology just like in a centralized database.

Chapter 12- Future of Blockchain

The popularity of the blockchain technology has increased, but most people are not sure what it is. The technology is expected to revolutionize the sharing economy. The fusion of blockchain technology and the sharing economy may create a revolution that will transform the economy and share the wealth beyond specific companies and individuals. This will have a great impact in the sharing economy now viewed as dead. The blockchain technology can unlock and energize the sharing economy by making it a bit cheaper to create and manage an online platform. Self-executing smart contracts can be used to coordinate transactions. This will ease the inequalities in today's sharing economy or overcome them.

The future of the finance industry may become dominated by the blockchain technologies. A global currency running on an efficient infrastructure will result in a massive reduction in costs for all participants and change global banking. Bitcoin is expected to revolutionize payments in the same way that email revolutionized communication. Central banks are expected to adopt the blockchain technologies and most financial transactions will be secured via cryptography.

Nasqad will start a blockchain-enabled digital ledger that will expand and enhance the equity management capabilities provided by the Nasdaq Private Market platform.

The settlement of equity, currency and fixed income trades through permissioned distributed ledgers provides a good opportunity for banks to create efficiency and new asset classes.

Scalability is expected to remain the holy grail of Bitcoin technology. Currently, Bitcoin technology is restricted to a sustained rate of about 3.3 percent because of Bitcoin protocol that restricts block sizes to 1MB. Scalability will remain the Holy Grail. Currently, Ethereum forms the best scalable blockchain platform.

The blockchain is expected to become a disintermediating world. People will come to understand that blockchain technologies are not simply an upgrade to databases and the Internet, but tools to re-architect social, political and financial systems. The Ethereum smart contract blockchain systems will invent near frictionless price discovery mechanisms for the purposes of intermediation. Intermediaries such as banks, notaries, custodians, accountants, trustees, agents will begin to find higher value propositions for customers since the trust cost will plummet. The net result will be a greater value for counter-parties of a particular transaction and less value to the intermediary.

Smart contract users understand the need for security. This has become an area of focus in smart contract best practices. There is also need for the auditing of smart contracts. Microsoft has formed the kinakuta, a smart contract audit and research working group.

Non-proof of work consensus algorithms are expected to be the new black. Casper will be the forthcoming direction for public the Ethereum network. Honey Badger, EtherMint and Hydrachain are good examples of Byzantine and non-Byzantine consensus mechanisms for various use case in private and permissioned environments.

Failures and consolidation may begin to occur in the blockchain because stakeholders may begin to see that their play-to-play consortia codebase does not have the network effects they thought it would have. Rapid implosions may be seen, especially in the permissioned blockchain infrastructure, where smart contracts are not supported, that compile to give executable EVM bytecodes.

A new regulatory environment is expected. Regulatory bodies will interact with the first class blockchain citizens such as Coinbase, ConsenSys, Coin Center and Union Square Ventures in order to understand and work together on a barely trodden next generation tokenized asset world. Ethereum developer tools are expected to improve, and the rate of software development will grow at an exponential rate.

Conclusion

You have come to the end of this guide. Blockchain technology is changing the way things are done. It is simply a decentralized, digitized, public ledger that records all cryptocurrency transactions. Records are added to the ledger in the form of completed blocks, and addition is done in a chronological order. The blockchain allows market participants to track all digital currency transactions without the need for central recordkeeping. Each node in the network has a copy of the blockchain that is downloaded automatically.

The good thing about blockchain technology is that the database is decentralized with no need for a central authority to maintain it. This is not the case with centralized databases. Banks and other financial institutions are now looking for ways to implement blockchain technology to help them carry out financial transactions. Each user participating in the blockchain plays a role to ensure that the database is in a consistent state. All the network nodes must come to a consensus for the database to be in a consistent state. For a consensus to be reached, previous transactions must be considered. This makes it hard for any malicious hacker to modify the blockchain data successfully. In short, blockchain technology has great potential. The technology is expected to dominate most aspects of human life including the financial sector in the near future.

Lastly, if you really enjoyed reading the book, please take time out to share your insights by posting a review on Amazon. It'd be really appreciated.

Thank you and good luck!
TJ Bernstein

www.ingramcontent.com/pod-product-compliance
Lightning Source LLC
LaVergne TN
LVHW052307060326
832902LV00021B/3745